16.95

Karate

'Highly recommended reading for
any aspiring martial artist.
This series will enhance your
knowledge of styles, history,
grading systems and finding and
analyzing the right club.'

*Stan 'The Man' Longinidis
8-times World Kickboxing
Champion*

PAUL COLLINS

This edition first published in 2002 in the United States of America by
Chelsea House Publishers, a subsidiary of Haights Cross Communications.

Chelsea House Publishers
1974 Sproul Road, Suite 400
Broomall, PA 19008-0914

The Chelsea House world wide web address is www.chelseahouse.com

Library of Congress Cataloging-in-Publication Data Applied for.

ISBN 0-7910-6555-3

First published in 2000 by
Macmillan Education Australia Pty Ltd
627 Chapel Street, South Yarra, Australia 3141

Text design and page layout by Judith Summerfeldt-Grace
Cover design by Judith Summerfeldt-Grace

Printed in Hong Kong

Acknowledgements
Photographs by Nick Sandalis, except p. 9 © Geostock.

The author would like to thank Sensei Brett Varga from Kushido Karate-Do
International, Caulfield Dojo, 6 Maple Street, Caulfield, Victoria, Australia.

**Techniques used in this book should only be practiced under qualified
supervision.**

Contents

What are martial arts?

Most people have seen at least one fantastic martial arts movie. A lot of it is trick photography. A **ninja** can not really jump backwards and land on the roof of a towering house! Then again, martial arts is about belief – belief in yourself and your ability to overcome any obstacle, no matter how big or small.

Ask any martial arts student why they train and the answer will be to learn **self-defense**. But that answer only scratches the surface of the term 'martial arts'.

One of the many functions of martial arts is to train students, both physically and mentally.

Martial arts has an ancient tradition that is steeped in discipline and dedication. Most martial arts have developed from ancient Asian combat skills. In **feudal** times, people in Asia had to defend themselves against attack. Quite often, peasants were not allowed to carry weapons, so self-defense became their weapon.

Some martial arts are fighting sports, such as karate and kung fu. Other martial arts concentrate on self-improvement, although self-defense is part of the training. These martial arts, such as judo and taekwondo, share the syllable *do*. Do means 'the way to **enlightenment**'.

Kung fu

Taekwondo

Judo

Dedication and discipline

Karate is hard work. Ask any senior student. On average, it takes at least three-and-a-half years (and that is if you pass every grading) to reach black belt standard, only to be told by your **sensei** that your journey has just begun.

Dedication plays a major role in the life of a martial arts student. Training can be up to four times a week, and an average session lasts from 60 to 90 minutes.

A student practicing simple moves.

Students practice one simple procedure over and over again. They might repeat a simple move 20 times in one night, only to repeat the same move the next time they train. Martial artists learn through repetition, so that even the most basic moves can be automatically performed when they are suddenly required.

Understanding karate

Karate is generally considered one of the heavier martial arts, as opposed to 'softer' martial arts such as judo and taekwondo.

Karate is a martial art that involves striking with the feet, hands, knees, elbows — in fact, every part of you is a weapon. A karate player, called a karateka, concentrates on putting as much power as possible into the point of impact of a strike.

*The **Yin and Yang** emblem is known to most martial artists. The Yin and the Yang represent the feminine and the masculine energies in martial arts. The Yin can be explained as flowing and fluid, as in performing patterns and good technique. The Yang might be the power and the ferocity of **sparring** with a partner. Martial arts need both opposing energies, the Yin and the Yang.*

The hands, balls of the feet, heels, forearms, knees and elbows are used to strike an opponent. Padded surfaces or wood are used to toughen up these areas during practice. However, timing, tactics and mental attitude are all considered just as important to a karate player as physical toughness.

Some styles of karate can be harsh. Senior students learn not to feel pain when receiving kicks and punches to parts of the body. It is believed that self-control is achieved when pain can be withstood without flinching.

There are several different schools of karate that use different techniques and training methods. Some karate techniques overlap with techniques from other martial arts. However, all karate schools teach the importance of respect for fellow players and instructors, and the importance of good mental attitude.

Japan: the birthplace of karate

Population:	126.2 million
Language:	Japanese
Currency:	Yen (¥)
Main Religions:	Shinto, Buddhism and Christianity

Japan leads the world as a fishing nation. This is because it is a nation of mountainous islands in the North Pacific Ocean. The four main islands are Honshu, Kyushu, Shikoku and Hokkaido, and they are situated off the mainland of east Asia. Tokyo, on the island of Honshu, is the capital city of Japan.

Many of Japan's mountains are active volcanoes, which often cause earthquakes. Mount Fuji is Japan's tallest mountain. It is 3,776 meters (12,390 feet) high and it is an extinct, or dormant, volcano.

The government of Japan is a democratic government, elected by the people. The head of government is the Prime Minister. The Emperor of Japan is the ceremonial head of state.

Kyushu

Shikoku

Pacific Ocean

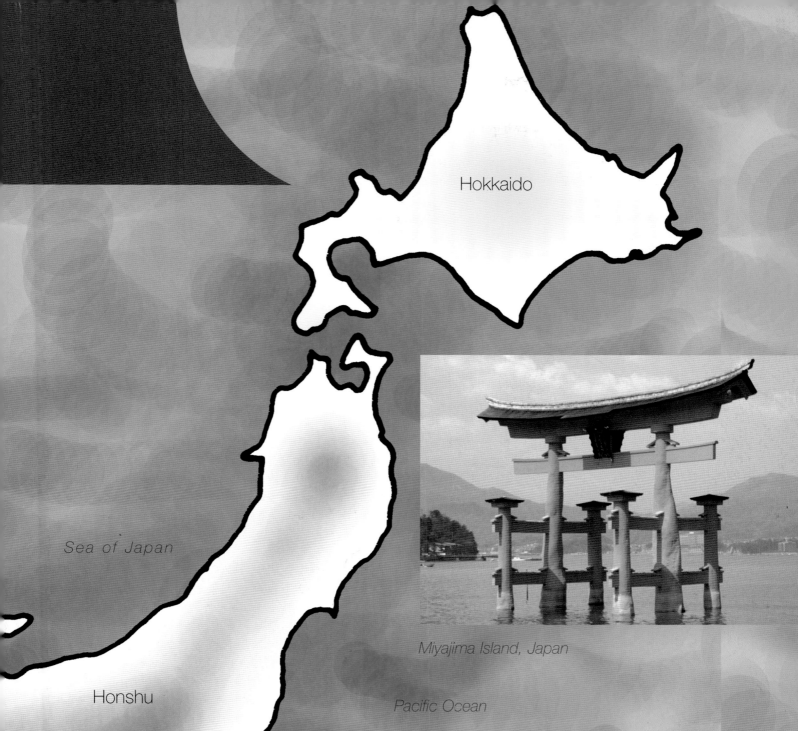

Hokkaido

Sea of Japan

Honshu

Miyajima Island, Japan

Pacific Ocean

Mount Fuji ▲   ■ Tokyo

In 1945, after Japan's surrender to the Allied Forces in WWII, karate and other martial arts were banned in Japan by the Allied Commission.

It's a fact!

The history of karate

Back in the 5th Century AD, Bodhidharma, a Buddhist monk from southern India, taught yoga techniques as a form of peaceful **meditation**. He travelled to China to establish a school of **Buddhism**, but his pupils were not fit enough, so he had to strengthen them. He did this by teaching them various fighting styles.

Karate was brought into Japan by Chinese traders who travelled to Okinawa and taught local fishermen.

Master Gichin Funakoshi (1867–1955), from Okinawa, introduced a new style of karate into Japan in 1922. Master Funakoshi's nickname was Shoto. He was experienced in the martial arts called kempo, tang hand and jujitsu. He combined these martial arts and called his combination style Shotokan karate. To this day it is the most popular of all karate styles. About one-third of karate students in Japan practice this style.

It's a fact!

Grandmaster Kanryo Higashionna (1851–1915) had such a strong stance that he would challenge four men to move him—all attempts were unsuccessful. It is said that after he performed his kata, the wooden floorboards would be hot where his toes had gripped the floor!

In 1925 Japan's first karate school, known as a **dojo**, was opened. Karate was not known in the United States until the 1950s, when American servicemen who had been stationed in Asia returned home. It was slow to take off, and did not really get going until Bruce Lee popularized kung fu in his films. Most Americans did not know the difference between kung fu and karate, so Bruce Lee was also promoting karate without knowing it!

Karate's most famous tournament fighters include Joe Lewis, Bill 'Superfoot' Wallace, Chuck Norris and Benny 'the Jet' Urquidez.

Dress code and etiquette

A karate uniform

Dress code

The karate uniform is called a karategi. Like most other martial arts uniforms, a karategi looks like loose-fitting white pajamas with a belt around the waist.

The karategi is made from cotton and is made to withstand training and contests. The belt passes around the waist twice and is tied in a reef knot so that it does not come undone during training.

How to tie your belt

① Hold the belt across your body, making sure the ends are of equal length on either side.

② Take the belt behind your back and cross it over once.

③ Cross the left end over the right end, at the front.

④ Tuck the right end under the belt around your waist.

⑤ Tie the right end over the left end (this is a reef knot).

⑥ Pull tight.

Etiquette

Karate schools require students to show proper respect for their sensei and dojo. Respect is shown by bowing.

- When entering a dojo, you should stand in attention **stance**, that is with flat hands against your thighs and heels together. Then execute a standing bow toward the most senior grade in the hall. You should bow again when leaving the dojo.

- When you approach an instructor, you should also bow as a sign of respect, and wait for a return bow before you start speaking.

- When receiving awards, certificates or medals, students bow to the principal instructor as well as the person delivering the award.

Other etiquettes to be observed are:

- It is considered bad manners to idly chatter or lounge against the walls.

- When students need to adjust their belt, they must turn and face the back of the dojo.

- Your uniform must always be clean and in good repair.

- When you enter the dojo, you must remove all jewelry, such as rings, necklaces, earrings and bracelets. This is to ensure the safety of both yourself and your training partner. Toenails and fingernails must also be cut short.

- When giving in to a hold that you are unable to break from, you should simply tap your opponent sharply with the flat of your hand. If your arms are pinned, you can submit verbally.

- Never take advantage of lesser **ranks**. This will not be tolerated in any martial arts club. It is considered bad form to injure anyone while practicing.

- Students should never distract other students who are training.

Bowing to an instructor

Group kneeling bow

Did you know?

Bowing is another form of shaking hands. It stems from Japanese feudal times when people bowed to show that they trusted the other person not to lop off their head with a sword. In the west, people shake hands, which initially proved that they did not carry a weapon in their right hand. This was a sign of good faith.

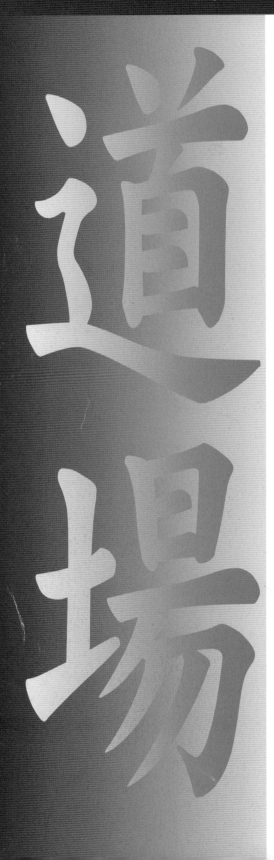

Before you start

Choosing a club

A look through the telephone book under the general heading 'Martial Arts' will show you where the nearest clubs are.

Different karate clubs teach different styles, or forms, known as **kata**. This means that you might join one karate club and be unable to train at another club because they practice a different style, or kata. Some clubs will claim that their style is the best. Have a talk to the head instructor and the students. The truth is, only you can tell which club you will be most comfortable with.

It is better to join a large club with many members. Also ensure that the club has students about your own age. If not, you could always join with a friend.

If money is a consideration, phone around and compare costs. They should not vary much. Some clubs have monthly charges, which can work out cheaper if you intend to practice at least twice a week. Other clubs charge a mat fee, or joining fee. Visitors normally do not pay, so it is a good idea to sit in on a session or two before joining a club. Some clubs even offer free introductory classes. As you advance through the grades, a grading fee is charged. Costs vary, depending on the level of grading. You are usually eligible for gradings every 48 hours of training.

Joining a martial arts club can be a lot of fun. Club members can sign up for competitions and travel interstate or even overseas to represent their club. Some clubs also organize weekend camps.

Clothing

It is not very expensive to start karate. Your first few training sessions can be performed in a sweatsuit, or loose pants and a T-shirt.

Before paying for a new karate uniform, visit second-hand or recycled clothing stores. Be sure to say that you require a karate uniform.

You could even ask the club that you are joining if any older students have uniforms that are now too small for them. This will also save you from having to buy the club's badges and sew them on.

If you buy your uniform new, be sure to order it one size too big. Despite what the manufacturer's label says, the uniforms do shrink. You will also need to purchase your new club's badges and the correct belt for your uniform.

As you advance, you will need items like arm and leg pads and boys will need groin protectors. Most specialty martial arts and sports stores will have everything you need. It is also a good idea to get a mouth-guard from your dentist. These items are especially advised for students who do a lot of contact sparring.

Insurance

Insurance is advised, although you are unlikely to get badly injured at a well-run karate club. Most clubs have insurance cover so it pays to ask.

Confidence and disabilities

Everyone feels nervous when they first enter a dojo under bright lights. Once you have passed your first few belt gradings — everyone passes the early belts — you will feel more confident. If you push yourself to face your fears, it will be easier to overcome them.

A light stretching work-out just before competition is a good way to keep warm and to loosen stiff muscles, which can cause nerves. Good instructors will teach you breathing techniques, which will calm you and help you to focus.

A disability should not stop you from trying karate. Many top athletes have **asthma**. Other athletes have **diabetes**. Getting fit through karate can help improve your overall condition. Just make sure your instructor knows of your complaint, take the necessary precautions and bow out when you do not feel well.

Fitness and training

Beginner martial artists are not usually ready for serious training. This takes time. They need to build fitness slowly. Most martial arts clubs have a beginners' class, where students learn the basic self-defense techniques and get fit.

Playing fitness games at training.

At the start of each training session, students bow to their instructor. A warm-up follows which involves stretching exercises. The instructor will then teach the class something new or ask the class to practice techniques already learned.

Contests are sometimes part of a training session, and some instructors pick teams to compete against one another.

Sparring

Sparring is when students pair off and exchange techniques with each other, usually without knowing their partner's next move. Sparring is practiced in training and it is a way of practicing moves that have been learned in kata. Sparring is not competitive as there is no winner or loser. The rules for sparring are set by the instructor.

Sparring

Full contact is not allowed in sparring, although injuries do occur if students do not have good control of their actions. Most clubs have protective equipment. Even so, the idea of sparring is to demonstrate your understanding of the techniques you are using. The aim is to work as a team, rather than against each other.

Stretching

As well as fitness you will need to gain flexibility. This means stretching all your body parts, especially your legs, to loosen tight muscles. The actor Ralph Macchio would not have been able to do those high kicks in *The Karate Kid* film if he did not have flexible hamstrings!

Do not be discouraged if you can not kick the top of a door. Most high kicks look flashy, but in a real fight situation martial artists rarely use them. This is because you are too easily unbalanced while kicking high, and the higher the kick, the less power you have. High kicking techniques are practiced more for coordination and balance, but are otherwise not practical.

Stretching has many purposes. It:

⊙   increases heart and lung capacity

⊙   helps you practice for the movements you are about to perform

⊙   helps avoid injury from pulled muscles

⊙   gives you greater flexibility.

It is important to keep each stretching movement gentle and slow. You should not use jerking or bouncing movements.

It is equally important to cool down after exercising. This maintains the level of blood circulation and reduces muscle spasms. Gentle cool-down stretches also help prevent injuries, because they reduce muscle tightness.

Karate techniques

There are dozens of kicks, punches and strikes to learn in karate. You will find some easier to master than others. But you should practice even the techniques that you do not like. It is also important to learn all techniques with both left and right hands and feet. It is equally important to learn how to defend yourself against various kicks and punches to both sides of your body.

Karate techniques are split into three main groups: breaking, striking and punching techniques.

Breaking techniques

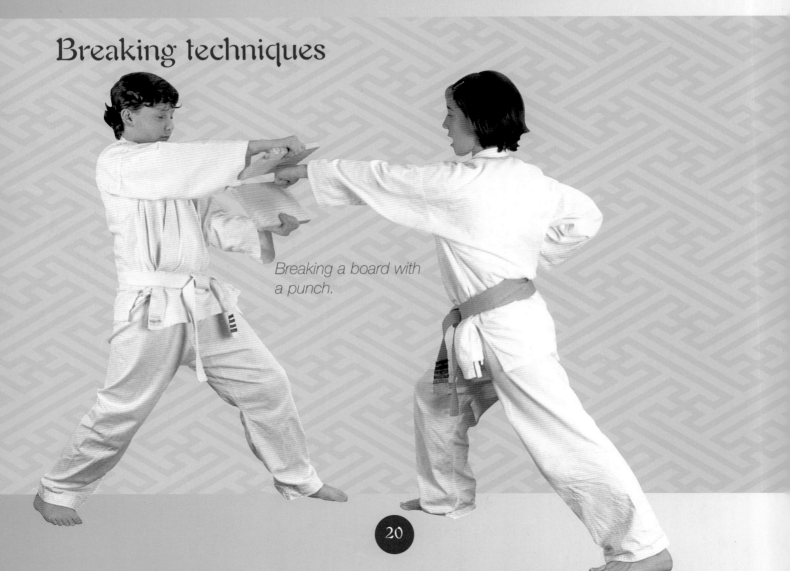

Breaking a board with a punch.

20

Richard Barathy is an American karate instructor who holds the world record for breaking fifteen 3.2 centimeter (1.3 inch) concrete slabs. This stunt was televised on the television show *That's Incredible.*

Breaking a board with a side kick.

Breaking is a demonstration of kicking and punching techniques.

Some karate schools practice breaking boards or roof tiles, although usually by senior students only. This is to minimize injuries. Breaking techniques are practiced to demonstrate a student's understanding of power. Some advanced students can break up to ten boards.

Breaking a board with a front kick.

Striking techniques

Hands and feet are used to strike. When striking, the student gives a kiai, or shout. This shout helps the student to focus and add force to the strike.

Spinning kick in three moves.

22

Pads are used to focus attention on an object while striking. They can be moved around to sharpen the attacker's reflexes.

Pad work

Punching techniques

Beginners learn simple punching techniques. To make a fist, tuck all your fingers into your palm, and then curl your thumb over your fingers so that it does not protrude from your fist. Always strike with the first two knuckles, because these are the biggest and strongest. Never bend your wrist when you strike. Keep your wrist in a straight line with your forearm.

How to form a fist.

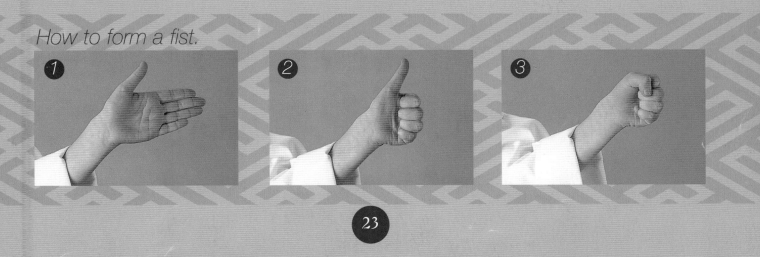

Kata

Kata are a sequence of techniques where students practice skills they have learned. The techniques learned by beginners are demonstrated in the first kata. Techniques in each kata are designed to practice defense and counter-attack. Some styles, like Shotokan karate, have more than 20 kata to learn. These form part of a student's training and development and are performed at gradings.

Kata are usually symmetrical, which means you end up where you started. Instructors can then check for evenness in your technique.

The student here demonstrates some of the techniques in the beginner's kata.

Self-defense techniques

The purpose of self-defense is to recognize and avoid dangerous situations. If a dangerous situation is unavoidable, students learn to unbalance their opponents in a controlled way.

Sweeping an attacker's leg from under them is a good and simple start. This is usually followed by a strike of some kind, or an armlock or headlock. The aim is to **immobilize** your opponent in the most efficient way possible.

Students learn to unbalance their opponents in a controlled way.

The belt system

The belt system showing the different color levels.

The color of a belt indicates the standard the wearer has achieved. Most martial arts have a belt system but the colors of achievement often vary.

In karate, white belts are worn by beginners and black belts are worn by masters. Grades in between wear other colors. There are generally nine or ten grades from white to black belt. A common sequence from beginner to advanced is white, yellow, orange, green, purple, brown and black. Stripes are added to each belt before a student moves on to the next color level.

Once you have reached black belt ability, you move on to dan grades. Dan simply means you have become a serious student. There are ten dan grades above black belt.

To achieve a higher grading, students have to perform kata. To reach black belt, students need to know many kata. They must show their understanding of every movement and execute it with focus and strength. Gradings for higher belts also include Japanese terminology, sparring and, in some clubs, board and tile breaking.

The language of karate

Most commands you hear in Karate are spoken in Japanese. It is a sign of respect to know Japanese. A karate player can also travel anywhere in the world and understand the language of karate.

To learn karate, you will need to know some of the following expressions. Some of the terms can vary from club to club.

dojo	training hall
kaisoku dachi	attention stance
karategi	training uniform
karateka	karate student
kata	forms or patterns of moves developed to improve technique by repetition
keri-waza	kicking techniques
kiai	translates as 'spirit harmony'; a shout, focusing on will and body, which gives force to a strike

kohei	a lower-ranking student	
nori	attention	
sempai	a senior ranking student (above your own grade)	
sensei	instructor	
shihan	master	
Shotokan	a karate style, developed by Master Gichin Funakoshi in 1922	
tsuki-waza	punching techniques	
uchi-waza	striking techniques	
yame	stop	

Counting one to ten

ichi	one	1
ni	two	2
san	three	3
shi	four	4
go	five	5
roku	six	6
shichi	seven	7
hachi	eight	8
ku	nine	9
ju	ten	10

Competition

Championships are held in big halls. The contest area itself is eight meters square (9.6 square yards). At the center of the square, there are two parallel lines spaced three meters (9.8 feet) apart. Contestants face one another on these lines. Judges sit in each of the four corners and award points. An arbitrator oversees all of the judges' decisions.

Contests last two minutes. During this time, contestants try to score points by striking, kicking and punching. When the referee calls yame (stop), the contestant with the most points wins.

Team events and kata competitions are also held.

Many clubs have their own tournaments, while some stage inter-club competitions. Other clubs do not promote competitive karate and choose not to enter tournaments.

Glossary

asthma	a breathing disorder
Buddhism	a religion that started in Asia
diabetes	a disease where the body does not fully take in sugar
dojo	training hall
enlightenment	well-informed
feudal	dating back to the Middle Ages
form	sequence of moves using specific techniques
immobilize	to hold still or stop movement
kata	forms or patterns of moves against an imaginary attacker
kiai	a shout which helps a karate player to focus and add force to a strike
meditation	thinking deeply and seriously
ninja	traditionally a spy or assassin
rank	the level of achievement that you have reached, i.e. the colored belt that you have earned
self-defense	usually grappling, which involves pinning your opponent so that they cannot strike you
sensei	instructor
sparring	exchanging techniques with a partner, usually without the partner knowing the next move
stance	a feet and leg position from which you can punch or kick
sweeping	unbalancing your opponent by hooking their foot
Yin and Yang	the two basic principles of the universe in Chinese philosophy. Yin is passive and yielding, whereas Yang is active and assertive

Index